Disciple or Partner?

A Profile of Charles "Tex" Watson

by P.O. Doe

About the author

P.O. Doe is a Probation Officer working in a major metropolitan area in the United States. He needs to remain anonymous due to privacy concerns and politics in the workplace. He has been working with the same agency for over a decade and has worked in more than ten different assignments within the department. He holds several college degrees, a requirement for some Probation Officer positions. He lives with his wife and family in a city that is a good distance away from where he works.

Contents

Behavioral Background

General Characteristics of a Profile

There are some basic factors that make up a profile. In the makeup of a mass murder offender, the exact etiology is unclear. It is the unique combination of the biology, the sociology, and the personal psychology of an individual, which accounts for the personality and thus the behavior of an individual[6]. But in their actions, there appears to be some basic similarities within the typologies. The five typologies used here for mass murder are the Family Annihilator, the Pseudo Commando, the Disgruntled Employee, the Disciple and the Set-and-Run Killer.

Some factors that are generally addressed in a profile are age, gender, race, motivation, anticipated gain, intelligence, spatial mobility, victim traits, victim relationship, and victim selectivity. Other factors to consider are precursor behavior or events, firearm ownership, abuse history and suicidal inclinations.

Factors such as age, gender, intelligence and race need no further definition. Motivation is what drives the killer and is divided into two basic types: intrinsic or extrinsic. Anticipated gain is what the person is expected to realize as an end to his actions, and is divided into psychological or material gain. Spatial mobility is the killer's proclivity to travel from their area of origin, and is divided into geographically stable or geographically transient. Victim traits are characteristics that the victims have in common, such as hair color or race. Victim selectivity is how the victim is chosen, and is divided into random and nonrandom. Victim relationship is how the killer knows the victim's, and is divided into affiliate and stranger[6]. Precursor behaviors or events are those that lead up to the event or trigger the event, such as loss of a job, relationship problems or talking about committing the crime long before hand. Firearm ownership refers to recent purchase of firearms or possible an obsession with them. Abuse history concerns the killers past history of being physically, sexually, verbally or psychologically abused or the killer's history of abusing animals or other people. The suicidal inclinations refer to the killer's will or plan to die[2].

Profile: Age

The age of the offender is different within the breakdown of type. Douglas and Olshaker[3] put the overall age as mid to late 30's to mid to late 40's. Yet when describing a Pseudo-Commando or assassin personality type of mass murderer, Douglas and Olshaker[3] state that the normal activation time for the event is in the offender's late 20's. Mendoza[9] describes the age of a mass murderer offender as young, without being more specific to numbers. Fessenden's[4] study of rampage killers places the average age at 34.2 years with the youngest at eleven and the oldest at 70. Levin and Fox[8] describe the mass murderer as being older than the typical murderer. They state only 15% of mass murderers are under twenty-five, in contrast to 45% of all homicide arrests being under twenty-five.

Profile: Gender

The gender of the mass murder offender is overwhelmingly male. Only five of the 55 mass murderers in Holmes & Holmes[6] were female. In Fessenden's[4] study 93% were male. Douglas and Olshaker[3] describe their typical mass murderer as male. Levin and Fox's[8] sample only one of 42 killers was female.

Profile: Race

The associated race of the mass murder offender is typically white. This is an area where mass murders differ significantly from other murders in the United States. Whereas blacks commit half the homicides in this country, only one in five mass killers is black[8]. The racial composition would seem to more closely approximate that of the population itself. Douglas and Olshaker[3] also infer that the race of the offender is in line with a country's racial makeup.

Profile: Motivation

The motivation of the mass murder is an element crucial in typology. A partial answer lies in the location of the motivation, either intrinsic or extrinsic[6]. With Disciple killers, the motivation is extrinsic as the leader commands an action. The motivation is also extrinsic for the Set-and-Run Killer, as the desire may be material gain for self or impacting the target's ability to make money. The other three typologies have something intrinsic as their motivation.

Profile: Anticipated Gain

The anticipated gain is another categorization factor. The gains are either psychological or material[6]. All typologies except the Set-and-Run Killer have anticipated gains being psychological. The Set-and-Run Killer, again, has basis in material gain.

Profile: Intelligence and Mental Illness

The intelligence of the mass murderer is a subjective factor. There are often articulate enough to be very comfortable with written communication, expressing their frustration and anger in letters to authorities and newspapers, as well as personal diaries[3]. Many have college degrees, but are unemployed[4]. They seem to have the intelligence to achieve, but have not been able to live up to that expectation. Intelligence does not seem to play as much of a factor as does mental illness in both Disgruntled Workers and Pseudo Commandos. Fessenden[4] found that more than half of all these type of killers had histories of serious mental health problems, these being identified as hospitalization for mental illness, a prescription for psychiatric drugs, a suicide attempt or evidence of psychosis.

Profile: Spatial Mobility

Spatial mobility is broken into two factors: geographically stable and geographically transient[7]. The Family Annihilator, the Pseudo Commando, and the Disgruntled Employee are typically geographically stable. They kill at or near where they live and/or work. The Disciple and the Set-and-Run Killer are more likely to be geographically transient. The Disciple will typically kill near the location of the leader. The Set-and-Run Killer is likely to include distance from the event as part of the pre-established escape plan[6].

Profile: Victim Traits

Victim traits are not an apparent factor. The victim is typically in the wrong place at the wrong time. As such, victim traits are non-specific for all five typologies[6].

Profile: Victim Relationship and Selectivity

Victim relationship and victim selectivity is a factor in the Family Annihilator and Disgruntled Employee typologies. The key to the Family Annihilator is killing his family. The Disgruntled Employee goes to his former workplace to kill, murdering those he used to know and work with. For the other typologies the victims are normally strangers and randomly chosen.

Profile: Other Factors

Other factors to consider are precursor behavior or events, firearm ownership, and abuse history. Precursor behavior includes: recent unemployment or a long period of unemployment; loneliness or depression; a family break up; troubles at work, including disciplinary actions; telling people what they are going to do before they commit the mass murder; and writing angry and frustrated letters to newspapers or public officials[9]. Firearm ownership to the point of obsession or recent obtainment of firearms[3] with predominant preference of semiautomatic weapons[4] is common. A history of abuse is also a common theme, either as the victim or the perpetrator[3].

Profile: Suicide Rate

For most of the typologies, suicide or death at the hands of police is the outcome of the mass murder event for the killer[6]. In Fessenden's[4] rampage killer study, 45% either tried to or did commit suicide and another 9% were killed by police. The exceptions are the Disciple, who desires to live on to please the leader, and the Set-and-Run Killer, who plans from the outset to escape.

With apparent increasing frequency, the public is given news via television and print of yet another horrendous crime of mass murder. Wilson and Wilson[12] contend that something has gone wrong in society that mass murder killers are multiplying at a high rate. Fessenden[4] does state the attacks are rare when compared to other American murders, but have provoked intense national discussion on crime, education and American culture. Dietz[2] notes that the definition of mass murder in itself eliminates more than 99% of violent crimes and thus makes mass murder an extremely rare social event.

As the size of the population of the United States grows, so do the overall number of murders. In 1900, the reported number of murders was 230. This is opposed to the reported number of 22,270 for 1989. The rate was 1.2 per 100,000 reported murdered in 1989[5]. So, the overall murder rate for the United States has increased, and with it, so has the rate of multicide.

Subject: Charles "Tex" Watson – Background

Copeville, Texas had a population of 150 people when Charles "Tex" Denton Watson arrived in this world on December 2, 1945[10]. Tex Watson was

the third child born to Denton and Elizabeth
Watson. He had two older siblings: sister,
Jeanne and brother, James. Watson's father,
Denton, was one of the most faithful church
members, working endless hours on the church
construction. Watson attended this little church
"every Sunday unless he was sick" according to
his mother, Elizabeth[10].

The Watson family purchased a building in 1936,
which still stands today. The little white framed
store, and residence located adjacent to it, are
still owned by the Watson family. This is where
Tex Watson grew up, in a small town with small
town people[10].

Watson spent his youth growing up like most
other boys. His high school days were recorded
in the local newspaper. He was a football player.
He played basketball. He earned letters in these
sports, playing four years in each one. He
worked on the Farmersville High School yearbook
staff[10].

A former classmate commented that Watson
cheated his way through high school. He did so
not just for passing grades, but for high grades.
The classmate cited Watson's low SAT scores as
evidence in contrast to his high grade-point
average[10].

Watson attended the United Methodist Church
and even taught a Sunday school class. Despite

this, before he graduated high school he had been introduced to the dark side of life: the Occult. Forbidden by the scriptures, he ignored the warnings. Watson opened himself up to the horrors of Hell[10].

One night Watson and two fellow athletes got a hold of a Ouija Board. The Ouija Board told the three friends that by the time they are twenty-five years old, one of them would be a doctor, one of them would be dead, and the other would be in prison[11]. This would come true.

There were not many places to spend your money in Copeville, Texas. It appears that Charles spent his time working in packing sheds, pumping gas at the store next door, or stocking shelves inside the rather antiquated family business. By the time Charles left for college, he did it in style. He had about $4,000 in the bank and a new car[10]. He seemed to be the all-American boy, scoring on and off the athletic field as often as possible. The money and the car got him attention and sex.

Watson had returned to Texas from California to be a pallbearer for his close friend, who died in Vietnam[10]. One of the last decent things he did before he became a killer! But it was a part of the prophecy that the Ouija Board had given him and his friends. One had died. Another was in medical school. That left Watson to go to jail.

Watson moved alone to college at the North Texas State University in Denton, Texas in the fall of 1964. Records show that he attended classes until the spring of 1967. He never quite fit in with the college crowd. The story is told that Watson stole some typewriters to gain acceptance into a fraternity. Records for fraternities show that no one by the name of Watson tried to pledge[10]. Likely it was another manipulation, as his mother bailed him out and paid for the damages.

While attending college, Watson got into using drugs. He became a dealer of drugs[10]. Driving drunk, wrecking cars, breaking into classrooms, using drugs, dealing drugs, Tex Watson chose his way of life[10].

The records show that Watson dropped out of school, without explanation. He moved to Dallas where he took a job with Braniff Air Lines. He was a baggage handler on the midnight shift. He lived fast and loose. Many people believe that he dealt drugs while working for Braniff. That job soon took him to Mexico, California, and Hawaii. He was moving in the fast lane, had all the sex he wanted, and no doubt learned how to sell drugs in all locations[10].

Although there was homosexual activity during his time with the Manson Family, we have no indication that he participated in homosexuality during his growing up years. Rumors are strong that he had sex with Manson, since sex was one of the ways Manson broke down the traditional values[1]. Either sex, both sexes, multiple sex partners, Watson seems to have participated in the Family without objection. Linda Kasabian, star witness for the prosecution during the trial, said that sex with Watson was animal like and left her with a feeling of being possessed[10]. It does not seem that there were many values to break down by the time Watson hooked up with Manson.

Tex Watson was a very gifted con artist, a masterful manipulator, and extremely dangerous before he joined up with Manson[10]. Watson, exposed to the occult, stealing, breaking and entering, dealing drugs, he was dirty before he ever met Charles Manson. Manson simply used the evil that was already inside of Watson to further his own demented goals[1].

From his writing we learn that he met Manson in the spring of 1968. In November 1968 he ran away from Manson, but he still continued to break the law[10]. He would be drawn back into the fold.

The United States Army was to be denied the service of Charles Denton Watson through his manipulation. Obtaining a letter from the doctor who did the knee operation from the car accident in January 1968, Watson was granted a medical deferment[11].

Watson went back to the Spahn Ranch/Manson commune in March 1969[10]. His reasons for returning are not clear, but one thing is certain about his return; he did not fear Manson. Everyone knew that no one left the Family, but Watson left anyway and he came back.

He worked on VW's and other stolen cars when he returned to Manson[11]. He not only listened as Manson told the followers how to kill Piggy; a name they used for anyone who they felt represented societal norms and the establishment. Watson taught tactics on how to kill Piggies by slitting their throats[10]. Watson even reputedly killed a man named Shorty Shea for Manson. Shea had allegedly been the informant who was responsible for the police raiding the ranch in August, 1969[10].

Watson describes in great detail during his trial the things he did when he returned to Manson. He says that Manson asked him to build him a house. Watson obeyed, and claims he worked on it from September until December 1968[11]. They did drugs, Watson lived in a tent by the creek, and the men enjoyed the sexual obedience of the female Family members. Watson tells us in court testimony that Manson often beat a female in the view of others to enforce obedience to his commands[10]. Watson's escapades of drug dealing, drug burning, sleeping around, mod clothing, and stolen girlfriends are all carefully hidden from the ears of the court[10].

In December 1968, Watson, calling from a phone booth, called a longtime friend to come and redeem him and Watson left Manson for the second time. From December 1968 to April 1969, Watson would be on his own. Perhaps he was swayed by the talk of Manson, but he was not at this time operating in fear of retribution for leaving Manson[10].

In the months before the killings, Watson consumed an amazing amount of drugs[11]. He followed the instructions of Manson. Most importantly, Watson totally rejected any value system for human life[10].

The driver was an eighteen-year-old who just happened to be in the wrong place at the wrong time. Watson startled the boy as he drove toward the gate. Steven Parent pleaded for his life telling Watson that he would tell no one. Without mercy, Watson fired four shots into the upper body of the first victim[10]. Sometime after midnight on Saturday morning August 9, 1969, the nightmare began.

The occupants of 10050 Cielo Drive in Benedict Canyon, home of famed film director Roman Polanski, were not aware of what had transpired outside the gate. Watson, Patricia Krenwinkel, Susan Atkins, and Linda Kasabian entered the property[1]. Watson gained access to the house by slitting a screen and then letting the women in through a door. Watson then sent two women to the back of the house to see how many people were there. There were four occupants: Sharon Tate, actress and Roman Polanski's girlfriend; Abigail Folger, heiress to the coffee fortune; Wojiceich Frykowski, film buff and confidant of Polanski; and Jay Sebring, former boyfriend of Sharon Tate[1].

Watson found Frykowski asleep on the couch. They tied him up then went for the others. Watson told the girls to bring the other three out

to the living room. Watson shot Sebring first[10].
Frykowski worked his way loose and tried to run.
He was stabbed repeatedly by Atkins, but kept
running. Watson pursued him and finished the
job[1].

When Folger also tried to flee, Krenwinkel
pursued her. By running out of the house, Folger
almost escaped over the fence. Krenwinkel, in
hot pursuit, delivered the deadly blows that
prevented her escape. Watson finished her off
and she died on the lawn[10].

The killers returned to the living room where the
very pregnant Tate was tied up. She begged for
her life and that of her unborn child. The killers
were not persuaded. Watson cut Sharon's face.
The cut on her face was not disfiguring. It was
more like a cat toying with a mouse before the kill.
Watson was brutal beyond description as he and
the others stabbed the other parts of her body –
several direct stabs into the heart, all fatal.
Sixteen times Sharon Tate was stabbed. She
was then hung while she was still alive. Any one
of the five wounds inflicted on Tate would have
been fatal[10].

Between the two male and two female victims,
not including the unborn child, 102 stab wounds
were delivered[10]. Neither money nor valuables
were taken. The killers strolled down the
driveway, but not before they wrote, "Death to

Pigs" and "Helter Skelter" in blood on the front door and a wall inside the house[1].

Tex Watson drove them down the hill, blood soaked and exhausted. They found a house with a lawn hose in the front yard and began to wash off. When confronted by the house's owner, Watson defended the group in an amazingly calm and polite manner. The owner of the house, a former law enforcement officer, suspected nothing[10].

The true trademark of a killer is death and destruction followed by calmness. A master manipulator giving the appearance of oneness with himself. Psychiatrists would later write that Tex Watson felt like he was just a good person but bad things happened to him[10].

Family members would later repeat the boasting of Tex Watson upon return to the ranch. Both at the ranch, and later at Myers and Barker Ranch in the high desert, Watson would tell how fun it was to trash the Tate house. Even when he was back home in Texas following the crimes, Watson would use the brutality of the killings to make his mother leave him alone. She believed that he could not have done it. Tex Watson told her how beautiful Sharon Tate was when he stabbed her. He has even referred to her as a "pathetic blond begging for her life."[10]

Watson, Krenwinkel, and another Family member, Leslie Van Houton, are recruited for a second night of slaughter[1]. This time Watson was ready to kill again. The all-American boy from a town of one hundred fifty people; the athlete, possessed and pathetic, killed again. This time with bayonet in hand, a larger, more brutal weapon[10].

On an early Sunday morning, Watson and the others piled into the car with Manson driving. He headed straight to the home of Leno and Rosemary LaBianca at 3301 Waverly Drive, in the Los Felix District of Los Angeles[10]. Those early morning hours brought the death of Leno LaBianca first. Rosemary was thrown on the bed, held in check by Krenwinkel and Van Houton. Hands behind her tethered about the neck with two lamp cords, one from each side of the bed[1].

In the next room, Leno was reasoning with Tex Watson. No doubt begging for mercy yet falling on deaf ears. Watson raised the bayonet, slashing and stabbing his victim[10]. Beckoned by the two girls, Watson goes into the master bedroom. Rosemary is still alive. The kitchen knives she had prepared meals with were not adequate for the killing of the owner. Tethered by the lamp cords, indecently exposed, lying face down, Rosemary is stabbed and slashed by Watson's bayonet. Raising the bayonet, he hits her spinal cord. Had she survived, Rosemary would have been unable to move. She was stabbed forty times in all[10].

Now dead, released from the ordeal of dying, Rosemary is again stabbed by Van Houton. Bathed in blood, Watson, Krenwinkel, and Van Houton continue their deadly deeds (Buliosi and Gentry, 1994). "Rise" is written on the wall of the living room. "Healter Skelter" is written in blood on the refrigerator, the misspelled word "Helter" was as it was written by the killers[10]. "Death to Pigs" was written on a wall and "War" was sliced across the stomach of Leno. To top it off, Watson and the girls used the LaBianca's bathroom to shower and then afterwards, ate snacks from their refrigerator[10]. Tex Watson (1978) says in his book, "Will You Die For Me?," that he patted the dog and walked out the back door.

The second night of slaughter had ended. The killers returned to Spahn Ranch sometime around sunrise. The trio then slept most of the day away[10].

Watson received a life sentence for the murders. He's still currently incarcerated and has become an ordained minister.

Tex Watson is a Disciple Killer type of mass murder. At age twenty-three when he committed the murders, Watson is outside the profile norm for age. Though the typology of Disciple killer is not directly correlated to an age bracket, Watson is outside the generic age given for overall mass murderers of mid-to-late-30s to mid-to-late-40s. He does fit the profile in being a White male.

In fitting with the profile, Watson's motivation was extrinsic. His leader, Charles Manson, commanded action. Watson did choose to respond to the motivation, as the case study shows that he was not afraid to leave the Manson Family as another option to killing.

The anticipated gain for Watson was partially within the profile. The psychological gain of maintaining Manson's approval, as well as the fear and respect of other members of the Family were definitely factors. But also was the material gain that Watson experienced as being a part of the Manson Family. He did leave and then came back twice to the Family, and Manson allowed him to do so. He came back for the hedonistic gains that awaited him there: money, drugs, sex, and power.

Though Watson did have to cheat to get high grades in high school and was not able to complete college, he is a fairly intelligent man. He is smart enough to easily manipulate a great number of people in his scams and drug dealing. Several years after he was caught, he wrote a book through dictating it to a minister. Not living up to an expectation was not an issue with this killer. Watson is the type to feed off others, and thrived in the opportunity that Manson gave him. Mental illness did not appear to be a factor, as there were no reported incidents or history.

The profile factor of spatial mobility was within the profile. Watson was geographically transient. He went to where the opportunities were. He went where the leader needed him.

Victim traits and victim selectivity were not within the profile. Manson apparently simply targeted "Piggies," or those that he felt represented the system, and sent his Family out to kill them. The victims were strangers to the Disciples and apparently chosen by Manson as representative of being "Piggies." The traits for what Manson decided as representative of someone who is a "Piggy" is unclear. The victim relationship was within the profile, as they had no relationship to the murderers.

Other factors in the profile to consider are precursor behaviors, firearm ownership, and abuse history. For precursor behavior, Watson did not really display traits common within the other typologies. He did not work other than to deal drugs and do what Manson directed him to. There were no reported family problems. He may have talked about the killings prior to the act, but probably only to other members of the Family. There are no reports of letter writing. Firearm ownership or recent purchase was not reported. Though a firearm was used as part of the killings, the weapons of choice were knives. This is within the typology profile for types of weapons used. A history of abuse is not indicated.

Also in keeping with the typology, Watson was not suicidal. He did in fact desire to live to kill another day, and did so when he and the others killed the LaBianca's on the second night. As such was the desire of the leader, to live on to kill more.

Summary

Watson fit well with the mass murder typology of Disciple Killer, meeting thirteen of the sixteen profile characteristics. He met the statistical expectations for gender (male), race (white), motivation (ideology), gain (hedonistically based), intelligence (high), spatial mobility (fled area), victim traits (random), victim relationship (none), victim selectivity (targeted as Piggies), precursor behavior (based around ideology and hedonism), firearm ownership (none) and (not) suicidal. He did not meet age, mental health, or abuse history. Admittedly, the information available to accurately assess these two of the three categories is limited. Mental health issues are suspected related to narcissism and psychopathy. Abuse history is unknown.

Tex Watson was a master manipulator. Although he does fit into the Disciple profile, it does appear that he was a step beyond the brainwashed flunky. He likely had a more substantial relationship akin to a partnership, but wasn't as charismatic and manically crazy as Manson. Call me a skeptic when I doubt his motivations in becoming a minister as being more about manipulating and controlling people than with actually changing and finding religion.

References

1. Bugliosi, V., & Gentry, C. (1994). <u>Helter skelter: The true story of the Manson murders.</u> New York: W.W. Norton & Company.

2. Dietz, P.E. (1986). Mass, serial and sensational homicides. <u>Bulletin of the New York Academy of Medicine, 62</u>(5),.477-491.

3. Douglas, J., & Olshaker, M. (1999). <u>The anatomy of motive.</u> New York: Scribner.

4. Fessenden, F. (2000, April 9). <u>Rampage killers: A statistical portrait.</u> <u>New York Times,</u> A1, A28.

5. Harrison, M., & Gilbert, S. (eds) (1996). <u>The murder reference: Everything you never wanted to know about murder in America.</u> San Diego: Excellent Books.

6. Holmes, R.M., & Holmes, S.T. (1992, March). Understanding mass murder: A starting point. <u>Federal Probation, 56(1),</u> 53-61.

7. Holmes, R.M., & Holmes, S.T. (1996). <u>Profiling violent crime: An investigative tool.</u> Thousand Oaks: Sage Publications.

8. Levin, J., & Fox, J.A. (1985). <u>Mass murder: America's growing menace.</u> New York: Plenum Press.

9. Mendoza, A. (2000). <u>The mass murderer hit list.</u> [Online]. Available: Wysiwyg://21/http://www.mayhem.net/Crime/murder1.html

10.   Nelson, B. (1991). <u>Tex Watson: The man, the madness, the manipulation.</u> Anaheim, CA: Pen Power Publications.

11.   Watson, C.D. (1978). <u>Will you die for me?</u> New Jersey: Revell.

12.   Wilson, C. & Wilson, D. (1995). <u>The killers among us, book II: Sex, madness and mass murder.</u> New York: Warner Books.

Disclaimer

The information contained in this book is for informational and entertainment purposes only. This book details the author's opinions about investigations, crimes, criminal behavior and the criminal justice system. The author is not licensed as an attorney and the information is not represented as legal advice. The thoughts and opinions of the author are purely his own and do not represent the opinions of any agency or entity within the criminal justice system.

Except as specifically stated in this book, neither the author or publisher, nor any authors, contributors, or other representatives will be liable for damages arising out of or in connection with the use of this book. This is a comprehensive limitation of liability that applies to all damages of any kind, including (without limitation) compensatory; direct, indirect or consequential damages; loss of data, income or profit; loss of or damage to property and claims of third parties.

The material in this book may include
information, products or services by third
parties. Third Party Materials are comprised of
the products and opinions expressed by their
owners. As such, I do not assume responsibility
or liability for any Third Party material or
opinions. The publication of such Third Party
Materials does not constitute my guarantee of
any information, instruction, opinion, products
or services contained within the Third Party
Material.

Acknowledgements:

I would like to make formal acknowledgements of the people who have inspired, mentored, motivated and helped me over the years. But, the circumstances that require my anonymity prohibit that. I am still grateful.

I am currently working on projects related the time I have spent in probation.   I am also working on other criminal justice topics related to true crime.

This Book is dedicated to my kids. You are the greatest joy I could ask for.

A lot of time and effort took place in not only writing each of the reports included in this Book, but in the creation of the Book itself. Please to not share or distribute without permission, but instead refer others to the website to purchase their own copy.

Please take the time to review this Book from the site you purchased it from!! I do read it and appreciate the feedback. Like any author, I do enjoy hearing from those who enjoyed the book!

I can be contacted (and followed) at the following locations:

My blog:
http://probationuncovered.blogspot.com/

Facebook:
https://www.facebook.com/probationuncovered

Twitter: @PODoe2015

Instagram: instagram.com/p.o.doe

Email: probationuncovered@gmail.com

Probation Titles Available from this Author:

Maximum Exposure: 42 Stories from Probation
http://amzn.com/B013NUJ8NS

Newbie Status: A Guide for Probation Officers to Navigate their First Five Years and Beyond
http://amzn.com/B014NF1EQ6

Left on Vacation Came Home on Probation: A Guide to Successfully Completing your Probation
http://amzn.com/B013N8T2YU

Gang Conditions: A Guide to Supervising Gang Members on Probation
http://amzn.com/B013N7D8BY

Sustained: Probation Internal Affairs Investigations and Your Rights
http://a.co/0wZJ0jw

On The Stand: Courtroom Testimony for Probation Officers
http://a.co/fagRuBQ

Just the Facts: Report Writing for Probation Officers
http://a.co/23InJpl

Fifteen 15 Minute Training Topics: Quick Training Topics for Probation Officers (Probation Training Topics)
http://a.co/1wEG43K

True Crime Titles Available from this Author:

The Woodchipper Murder: The Forensic Evidence
Trail in the Homicide of Helle Crafts
http://amzn.com/B013N6DYDM

Set and Run: A Profile of Timothy McVeigh
http://amzn.com/B015F9S908

96 Minutes of Hell: Shots from the Tower
http://amzn.com/B013N8BCIO

Disciple or Partner: A Profile of Charles "Tex" Watson
http://amzn.com/B0163JNEEK

Disgruntled: A Profile of Joseph Wesbecker
http://amzn.com/B01652QUGY

Annihilator: A Profile of John List
http://amzn.com/B0163WTU54

The Killing Frenzy: Profiling Mass Murder
http://amzn.com/B0163JZG0U

Messy Murders: Death and Dismemberment by
Chainsaw
http://a.co/d/b9AfkcV